Sort

with God

Living as a Teen Today

Jim Auer

LIGUORI
PUBLICATIONS

One Liguori Drive
Liguori, Missouri 63057
(314) 464-2500

Imprimi Potest:
John F. Dowd, C.SS.R.
Provincial, St. Louis Province
Redemptorist Fathers

Imprimatur:
Monsignor Edward J. O'Donnell
Vicar General, Archdiocese of St. Louis

ISBN 0-89243-163-6
Copyright © 1982, Liguori Publications
Printed in U.S.A.

.

Cover Photo: H. Armstrong Roberts
Cover Design: Pam Hummelsheim

Chapters contained herein originally appeared in the LIGUORIAN
magazine under the heading "Under 21." Our thanks to the editors
of the LIGUORIAN for their kind permission to reprint these articles
as they appear here.

TABLE OF CONTENTS

TABLE OF CONTENTS

1

Thinking of Dropping Out
of the Church?

I have a friend named Dan. He's a wonderful guy —
friendly, helpful, usually pretty smart. A few weeks ago he
tried to drop out of his house.

I don't mean he tried to jump out of the attic window or
anything like that. I mean dropping out in the sense of giving
up on something. When people drop out in that sense, they
usually believe they are trading for something that seems
easier or more fun or both. People drop out of school, out of
jobs, out of a lot of things. Dan almost dropped out of his
house.

You see, he got it into his head that he was spending too
much of his time and effort and even money on the upkeep of
his house, and that the fun of living there had gone away. He
had his eye on a brand new house that would cure all those
headaches.

What Dan Saw

"Take this yard, for example," he said. "Look at the time I
spend trimming bushes, cutting grass, all that stuff. In the
new place I would have a lot less to do."

Dan has a backyard you could fall in love with, even if
you're not exactly into yards in a big way. It is a deep, wide
expanse of lush grass, dotted with fruit trees, bordered by

flowers, and enclosed by tall, thick hedges and bushes. I envy it every time I see it. So do lots of other people.

Dan was right. It took a lot of work to maintain that yard, whereas at the new place . . . well, there would be very little yard to keep up. It is an ordinary square with ordinary-looking grass; it has no trees, no bushes, no flower beds. It looks out on a half dozen other yards exactly like it.

The yard wasn't Dan's only complaint. To hear him talk, you would think his house must also be a wreck or a freak or something of each. In his opinion, some rooms were too big and others were too small; the kitchen needed new tile and the house needed another bathroom; in a couple of years, the gutters would have to be replaced.

All Dan saw were the defects — and a new home was going to solve all his problems.

Poor Eyesight

But it is like that when we are tempted to drop out of anything. A weird sort of filter slips over our eyes; all we see are the bad points (real or imagined) of where we are, and the good points (real or imagined) of where we think we would rather be.

Let's take the Church, for example. When people think of dropping out of the Church, they see only the defects.

"If the Church is so great, how come . . . ?"

"If religion is so important, why is religion class a drag?"

"If worship is supposed to be joyful, why are some of the hymns so slow and boring?"

The list goes on and on: Father's sermons are too long and mean little or nothing to me; Sister has a quick temper; the Pope doesn't seem to understand this or that; the religion teacher has a personality like stale sausage; the parish doesn't have sense enough to air-condition the church and the school; the parish doesn't have teen dances.

Suddenly, it seems almost easy to conclude that if God is perfect, he couldn't possibly be behind all this. Then another tempting idea creeps up: "Hey, look at all the rules and stuff you can get rid of — if you drop out! If you don't belong to something, you don't have to keep the rules."

So what does such a person become? An atheist? A God and Church hater? No. ("I still believe there's a God and all that but . . . .") He or she becomes a dropout.

A Perfect Church?

There are probably as many reasons for dropping out of the Church as there are people who do so, but the majority of such dropouts most likely could be listed under one heading: "The Church Isn't Perfect."

It isn't? The Church established by Jesus Christ? And guided by the Holy Spirit? You are admitting this right here in public? What about that guarantee of infallibility you've heard mentioned in your religion class?

The guarantee we have is that the Church will never officially teach something that would lead us astray in regards to God's truth. And that is most reassuring, if we stop and think about it. But as for the *people* (like ourselves) in the Church, it's a different story. Sometimes we expect more perfection from them than they can deliver. Jesus promised to be *with* his Church until the end of time. He did not promise to zap all its members, or even all its leaders, and suddenly make them one hundred percent wise and wonderful and thoroughly cool *before* the end of time.

In all fairness, we ought to have at least as much sympathy and understanding for the Church as we do for anyone else. If, for example, a favorite rock group has a couple of bad cuts on their new album, we are not going to throw out all their old ones and never listen to them again. Nor do we quit a ball team because one of the coaches calls (as we see it) a dumb play now and then. If the Spanish teacher is really a decent guy and does what he can to help, but has an occasional boring class, it's not quite fair — or smart — to call his whole course the pits and stomp off.

I am not saying that the Church is no different and no better than any other organization, or that it turns out mistakes like Kelloggs turns out cornflakes. That's not true.

A Pilgrim People

The Second Vatican Council described the Church (us — you, me, Pope John Paul, and a few million other people) as a "pilgrim" people . . . on a journey, struggling together. People can drop out of the journey — there is no tour guide holding a gun at anybody's head — and when they do, it might seem like they have made a break for freedom or independence or a more carefree life (like Dan thought he was going to do with the new house). What they do not see until much later (sometimes never) is that when they drop out of the journey, they step off pretty much in the middle of nowhere.

Dan? He finally decided that even though his beautiful old house wasn't perfect, it was where he belonged. Last time I saw him, he was putting new tile in the kitchen and adding another bathroom.

That's something like the Church. It's not perfect. But then we — you, me, Pope John Paul, a few million other people, and the Holy Spirit — aren't finished working on it either.

2
The Drinking Decision

I'll call him Barry, although that is not his real name. He was in my classroom a few years ago. He studied, participated fairly well, turned in OK work, and earned passing grades. I really liked him. I still do.

Today Barry is in trouble. He is on his way to becoming an alcoholic. Maybe he's already there.

And maybe you are thinking, "Hold it. I've heard that before. It's called: 'Young People Shouldn't Drink Because They'll Mess Up Their Lives, Lose Their Religion, and Turn Out Rotten.' And as usual, it begins with a horror story about a kid who is burnt out from booze."

I can understand the feeling. That particular sermon, complete with scare technique, has made the rounds often enough. I will also admit that it is usually given by adults who are more familiar with beer and bourbon than they are with kids.

But stay with me.

Barry and the Bottle

There is no horror story connected with Barry. He has never passed out in the gutter with a wine bottle in his hand. He has not dropped out. He is not bumming or hanging around or getting busted now and then.

He is still in school, still plays sports, gets passing grades, and a lot of girls think he's cute. Barry is not burnt out. There is no horror story . . . yet.

But Barry's grades are not really what they could be and there are at least two girl friends who do not think he is cute when he gets polluted — which is happening more frequently. He has come close to totaling his car and maybe killing a couple of friends. Even Barry isn't too eager to talk about that.

His whole life could go down the bottle. Perhaps it won't — but it could and it is getting more likely every day.

I know that and so do several other people, including his former girl friends. The trouble is, Barry doesn't know it.

Does Barry think alcohol is completely safe? that it never hurts anybody? Of course not. He is not a screaming idiot. Nobody thinks "Alcohol can't mess anybody up."

But almost everybody thinks "Alcohol can't mess *me* up."

That's the kicker, and it is pure fact: Nearly every person who gets messed up from alcohol thinks either "I don't have a problem" or "I can handle it."

When Does the Problem Begin?

"Why are people always bugging young people about drinking?"

That is a good question. It's not that young people are not as smart as adults or that they drink more than adults do or that their drinking causes more problems. And it is certainly not that drinking is a more serious moral problem just because a person is young.

But as a young person, you have an advantage over seasoned drinkers. You still have time to decide on a personal program of safe alcohol use or nonuse — before a problem arises. Because once you have the problem, you are never going to admit it. That is exactly how it works.

When does a drinking problem begin? It's hard to say, really. It's like asking "When does a person begin to fail a course?" Obviously, it started long before the final grade was printed.

But precisely when? with the first missing or half-done assignment? with the first cut class — or maybe the third? Frankly, it is almost impossible to pinpoint.

In some ways, it's like catching a cold. You start with a sore throat. Sometimes that is all that happens, but sometimes it goes all the way. You get a headache; you can't breathe; your eyes water; you ache all over — the whole bit. At what exact point could you say for sure "I'm going to have a terrible cold"?

It's like that with a drinking problem — with one difference: A cold will eventually go away by itself. A drinking problem never goes away by itself. Never.

Be Honest with Yourself

Once you have a drinking problem, it is simple to "prove" you don't have one. There are dozens of ways to do this. Here's one you might use:

"People with real drinking problems are messed up. I'm not messed up. I'm not flunking out. I've got a job, and I've never been busted. I go to church on Sunday. I help the old guy next door shovel snow and I don't even ask for money. When you come down to it, I'm really a good person. I'm making it. So I can't have a problem with alcohol. If I did, I wouldn't be such a nice person."

I wish that were true. It would be great if passing courses, holding a job, going to church, and being nice could guarantee that you do not or will not have a drinking problem. Or that all these things could somehow make everything OK for you and keep anything bad from ever happening.

But most of the time the "drunken bum" who kills three people on the highway is a nice person who loves his or her family, or a nice kid who really tries in school. Drinking problems just cannot be reasoned away that easily.

Some People Make It

There are two important things to remember: (1) If you believe alcohol could never mess up your life, you already have something in common with every person who's ever gotten messed up with it; and (2) every alcohol-troubled person functions or "makes it" — sometimes rather well — for awhile.

How long that while lasts is an individual matter. Every person's body chemistry reacts differently to alcohol. In some people it can build up an addiction with frightening quickness; in others the process is more subtle. This is completely beyond one's control.

Consequently, some people go from their first drink to become total wrecks in a year or two, while others can drink quite a bit for quite awhile without the damage becoming obvious. Everybody, of course, wants to think that he or she is exactly like the latter.

There are several things wrong with this comparison. First, the seemingly unharmed person may not be "making it" as well as it looks on the outside. He or she may be incredibly messed up on the inside or have relationship problems that do not appear on the surface. Second, even if appearances are true, the ability of one person to tolerate alcohol has nothing to do with another person's reaction to the same drug.

You Don't Have to Drink

The bottom line in all this is that when it comes to alcohol, you have to make some decisions — ahead of time.

First, you must decide whether or not you really want to drink at all. You don't have to, you know. You are perfectly normal if you really do not care for beer, wine, bourbon, gin, or anything else — even though a lot of people equate drinking with being adult, fun-loving, popular, or generally "with it." Nobody should have such power over you that his or her opinion would make you drink when you do not want to.

True, you will have pressure from peers. (Adults experience it too, by the way.) But many young people have discovered that they can hold firm to their guidelines on drinking without becoming social outcasts. I am not saying there won't be any pressure — I am saying you can survive it. You can be accepted by your friends with or without drinking (*unless* drinking is the only or the main thing that brings your group together). It is simply a matter of not giving in the first couple of times somebody makes a sarcastic remark or asks what's the matter with you.

Do you let others tell you that you *have* to like biology better than history? that you *have* to play soccer? that you *have* to style your hair a certain way? I think not. Then don't let others tell you that you *have* to drink, either.

Another thing about being a nondrinker that can be difficult is finding a different way home if the person or persons you're with have had too much to drink. This is called self-preservation. You don't have to *be* a drunk driver to end up dead or crippled. Riding with one will do the job just as effectively.

No Harm?

"But a lot of adults I know of drink like . . . ."

Right! Adults also jump off bridges, rob little old ladies, and start wars.

"But still, when you come down to it, there's no harm in getting a little smashed every now and . . . ."

Barry thought that, too. He still does. That's the whole bit in a nutshell: Once you've got the problem, you don't want to admit you've got a problem.

But you still have time to draw up some guidelines for yourself — ahead of time.

Some people like skydiving. It's not for everybody, but some people enjoy it. It is also potentially very dangerous. But skydivers with any sense at all know *before* they jump *exactly* how far they will go until they will open their parachute and end their free fall. Otherwise they could end up — to put it mildly — very messed up.

Drinking is a lot like that. It would be very smart — to put it mildly — to know ahead of time what is involved and how far you can safely go.

3

Superteen

Ralph Waldo Emerson said, "Hitch your wagon to a star." The Army advertisements tell you to "Be all that you can be." Even a beer commercial encourages, "You only go around once in this life, so reach for the gusto."

You also hear pep talks incorporating ideas such as "Dare to be different," "Don't be satisfied with being average," and "You can do anything if you want to bad enough and try hard enough."

And parents occasionally say something like "We want to see you really make something of yourself."

This is all OK and chances are it is well-meant advice — usually from people who have your best interests at heart. It is worth listening to and thinking about. Unfortunately, it can also send you on a real guilt or anxiety trip. It can make you feel like you have to be Mr. or Miss Superteen in order to be anybody.

Miss Superteen is a member of the National Honor Society, plays varsity volleyball, had a lead part in the spring play, works on the staff of the yearbook, and represents her class on the Student Council. She is a member of the Teen Fashion Board at a leading department store, is completely liberated, yet makes a fantastic pineapple cheesecake, holds down a part-time job, and does volunteer work at a local orphanage.

Mr. Superteen is also a member of the National Honor Society, plays varsity soccer and baseball, is chairman of two student committees, and stars on the debating team. He works out on Nautilus equipment four times a week, recently won both an essay contest and a motorcycle rodeo, plays lead guitar, holds down a part-time job, and will have his choice of several scholarships to leading universities.

Both, of course, are immensely popular with their classmates and win the admiration of adults wherever they go.

Maybe there is a Superteen in your life. He or she may be a real classmate who seems to fit the description or an imaginary composite, such as we have mentioned. In either case, Superteen seems to be accomplishing more than you are. You look at Superteen and then you look at yourself; the comparison can send you on a real downer. You are not "doing and being it all," as he or she seems to be. In fact, you look depressingly ordinary. As a result, you are easily tempted to conclude, "I'm not worth too much," or even "I'm sort of a failure."

You do not say that to anyone, of course, or go around wearing "I'm Nobody" buttons. In fact, outwardly you may be saying something like "Who wants to get into a thousand different things like that?" Inside, though, a little guilt-tape clicks on and scolds, "Oh, but you should. You should do all those things. 'Be all that you can be,' remember?"

Now if it sounds like I'm putting down ambition, hard work, achievement, and excellence, please hang on. That is not my point at all. I also believe in "being all that you can be" — correctly understood.

There can be a harmful conflict between the two pictures mentioned above: the picture of yourself as you think you should be (Superteen or something like it) and the picture of yourself as you think you are (ordinary, not quite good enough).

Imagine these two pictures as two chemicals that can be dangerous when combined. I can think of at least three unhappy results of their combination.

1. You can become a member of the MAD SCRAMBLERS. The Mad Scramblers not only feel they should "be and do it all," but they are also convinced that they can — if they just push a little harder. Sometimes they are quite successful in many different activities, but sometimes they have to pay too big a price for it. They have little or no time to make friends or appreciate the world in general, no time to think about where their life is going or where they want it to go. They may even be laying the foundation for becoming "workaholics" (which is a real thing, by the way). Sometimes they are spread too thin to reach success in any one thing. Or perhaps something important suffers (like grades) because so many other things are fighting for time in their life.

2. You can become one of the (GEE, I'M SORRY) AVERAGE KIDS. These individuals don't try to be and do it all, usually because they know they can't — but they still feel bad about it. Maybe they don't go out for football because they are five feet five and a hundred twenty-three pounds, but they feel they ought to be six one and one hundred eighty and on the team. They work hard for C's and B's but feel a really worthwhile person would be getting A's.

3. You can join the QUITTERS' club. The Quitters look at Superteen, look at themselves and say: "No way can I ever be like that!" So they give up on the idea of working for any measure of success. It's an "if I can't have it all, why bother with anything" attitude. So they really do settle for being far less than they could be. And often the quitter becomes sour and cynical about others who are successful in any way: "He just does it for show." "She got the award because she butters up the teachers." "Big deal!" "Who cares?"

How do you avoid these traps or know if you are in one?

Nobody Does It All!

If you suspect yourself of becoming a Mad Scrambler, check out these questions: Are all your activities YOUR ideas or did someone tell you, "You really ought to . . . ."? Do you really, deeply want to do them or are you imitating or trying to keep up with somebody else? At the end of a day, are you generally happy and at peace with what you have accomplished or do you nearly always feel it wasn't enough?

Hey, nobody does it all. Nobody. There isn't time for everything in anybody's life.

When Shane Gould, the Australian swimmer, was in her teens, she had a rather extreme goal: to be the best in the world. Her basic ability indicated that it might happen given enough work, and she wanted to try for it. And she made it.

If you read her training schedule, you begin to understand why. Every minute of every day was scheduled and accounted for, beginning at 4:20 A.M. As you might guess, almost all her time fell into one of three categories: school, sleep, and swimming. This could have created a huge problem if becoming the world's best swimmer had not been her own personally chosen goal, or if she had had delusions about accomplishing a half dozen other major things along with it. But she knew it would require virtually every available waking minute, and to her the sacrifice was worth it.

She became the world's best swimmer. But she did not do all the things she might have. And that's OK. It's OK for you, too. Not only OK, it's the way things are: Choosing to do one thing eliminates another — sometimes lots of others.

Appreciate Yourself

"But I'm just . . . me." The (Gee, I'm Sorry) Average Kid forgets an important fact: Some accomplishments attract attention, even make the newspapers — but that does not necessarily make those accomplishments worth more. If, for example, you break the city record for the high jump or get named to the Teen Fashion Board, you will probably get your name in the papers, maybe your picture, too. And that's a neat thing. Not everybody can or does do that. Be really proud of it.

But if you give up a weekend or more to help your grandfather clean and fix up his house or if you regularly, uncomplainingly help your parents with the house and the yard work or if you help a friend who is having trouble with algebra prepare for a test, you will definitely not get your name in the papers. There are thousands of things like this — and are they really less important or less worthwhile than something that may get your name into the public eye? Of course not.

You probably have run up a whole string of qualities and accomplishments without fully recognizing them. Start counting them. Appreciate yourself. God does. (I sometimes visualize God throwing his arms up in divine exasperation at many of us and saying, "Peter, you know what their problem is? Their problem is they don't see how neat they are most of the time. I made each one of them unique and special — and they walk around feeling ordinary.")

Don't Give Up on Yourself

If someone has simply quit, given up on really using his or her talent, it is usually easy to tell. For starters, there are probably a number of qualified, level-headed people who see it.

If your life seems full of teachers, counselors, parents, and relatives all saying, "You could do so much more if you tried harder," you just might consider that there may be some truth in the message. It is also good to remember that people who use their ability are just plain happier than people who don't. And happiness is, after all, the bottom line. A pretty smart man named Saint Thomas Aquinas said that a little over seven centuries ago.

Often someone who is just bumming or just getting by feels that he or she has already wasted too much time, too many opportunities. "I already blew it, so why start to try now?"

There is a reason why we have the old saying, "It's never too late." Do you want to know why? Because it *is* never too late, that's why. Because it is simply true. It might be too late for one opportunity, but not for others.

Colonel Harlan Sanders retired at sixty-five, feeling he hadn't accomplished much, and by many standards he hadn't. He decided to do something about it, despite the fact that he was already sixty-five. He tore up his first Social Security check, and then went on to found Kentucky Fried Chicken. Now it isn't the smartest thing to wait that long to put some real push into your life, but the story does prove a point.

And if God can make an Easter out of Good Friday, he can certainly help you give your life a fresh start if it needs one.

Check It Out

The next time the idea of being a Superteen crosses your mind, check out the really strong possibility that you already *are* a Superteen. Pin a little mental medal on yourself. There is nothing wrong with that, as long as you do not stop putting out effort afterward.

And if you think you still need a lot of growth, or if you are wondering which way (or how many ways) to grow in, check it out with God in prayer. After all, you are his idea — and it always helps to consult the manufacturer's directions.

4

The Real Meaning of Sex

A person I once knew kept a Christmas tree up all year long (an artificial tree, obviously). Ornaments and lights, tinsel and icicles were never taken off. The tree stood in a small entrance hallway. At Christmastime, it was moved into a corner of the living room and the colored lights were turned on. Otherwise, there was no difference between Christmas and any other time of the year. Whenever people went in or out of the front door, they passed the Christmas tree.

It is difficult to see how that tree could have anything special to give to the Christmas season.

The more special or valuable something is, the more we reserve it for special people, special times, special occasions. If you own a diamond necklace, you do not wear it to a picnic. If you get a personal letter from your favorite movie star, you don't leave it on a pile with yesterday's newspapers. If you own a classic '66 Mustang with a plush, customized interior, you don't use it to haul topsoil or run a taxi service. That's the way it is and should be with special things.

Sex in the Media

With that idea of specialness as a measurement, a lot of people out there do not think much of their sexuality — or yours or anyone else's, for that matter. Hundreds of stories, television shows, and films tell you, directly or indirectly, to use your sexuality in any way whatsoever and whenever the opportunity presents itself. Dozens of assorted "Do it" T-

21

shirts and bumper stickers tell you the same thing about your body: It's cheap — nothing special about it. Just use it any chance you get.

I hope you are smart enough not to buy that.

The media can make things that are far from commonplace or widespread *seem* that way. Advertisers, for example, know the power of the "bandwagon" effect. If they can convince people that "everybody" is buying their product, lots of otherwise intelligent people will rush out and buy it — whether or not they need it and whether or not it is worth the price.

Something like that is happening in the way the media present sexuality. The picture coming across is that "everybody does it." Right, wrong, and commitment to the other person don't seem to matter much anymore.

As a matter of real fact, that isn't so. Ann Landers learned this one time when she printed a statement that most eighteen-year-old males would take anything a girl was willing to give plus whatever else the guy could talk her out of. Ms. Landers was absolutely deluged with letters from guys (and their girl friends) saying, "No way — a *lot* of guys are *not* like that."

But in the meantime, many people are hearing only the other message. Unfortunately, some of them — even some kids who should know better — have come to the conclusion that casual sex is the order of the day.

Why wait? Is sex so bad? No! You wait because sex is so good. Sex is so good it deserves (like the Christmas tree) its proper setting — the way God planned it. (It really *was* his idea, remember?) Sex is *so* good in a setting of "with you only . . . forever" that people who move in and out of bedrooms and vans — as though they had revolving doors — have no idea what they have missed. There is a really dumb idea around that faithful married couples share sex out of routine, and that only the swingers really tap the full, exciting enjoyment of sex. Sorry, but it is the other way around. Trying to find the true meaning and experience of sex in casual, temporary encounters is like trying to capture the true feeling of Christmas on a hot, muggy day in the month of July. You need the real setting to make the real experience possible.

Sex Has Something to Say

It is always a good idea to think before you say something . . . to make sure it is what you really want to say and that you won't regret having said it. That applies to sexuality, too.

Because sex is communication, sharing sexuality always SAYS SOMETHING. It might say something terrific and it might say something gross. But it *always* says *something.*

Unfortunately, in the wrong setting sex can say some not so great things. Here are some of them. If they seem rather negative, well, maybe it's because sex in the wrong setting can be rather negative.

"I want a reputation. I want people to envy me as a man or as a woman. You are a trophy that will impress people."

"I want to feel needed and liked, but I'm not too sure that I am likeable and worth something. So I'm rewarding you for paying attention to me. I hope you will pay attention to me again sometime."

"I'm not completely sure of myself. I need to prove that I'm not just a little kid anymore. Your body should be fairly good proof."

"My friends are putting pressure on me to score with somebody. You're it."

"I feel like lashing out, like breaking some rules. Your body is a convenient place to break some rules."

"Fun is what life is all about, so let's do each other a favor, OK?"

Sound bad? Really gross is more like it. But those are not the ideas to concentrate on. Remember, the same thing often has the power to create both good and bad, both beauty and horror. Fire and water, for example, can either sustain life or wipe it out.

So if those "messages" of sex in the wrong setting strike you as ugly, think what a beautiful message sex in the right setting can give.

It says "I love you — completely, unreservedly. From among all the people on earth, I choose you to give everything I have, to give the very deepest, most precious part of me; and I trust you with it.

"I want to be one with you, and only you, forever — because there is no one else in the world like you."

Few things can even come close to the beauty of that message. But what makes it terrific? The "only you" part, that's what. You just cannot send that message to several people, not without destroying the message itself. If you try, it comes out, "I give myself totally, completely, everything I have, only to you — and a few others."

Not quite the same, is it?

Why Wait?

I've sometimes heard people talk about sex simply in terms of "before marriage it's dirty and bad, but afterwards you're allowed to."

Wow! What a tragedy if someone goes through life with such a narrow, shallow vision of such a beautiful part of being human. Among other things, it makes "waiting" seem like nothing more than a stern discipline you have to endure, with no real value to it except to avoid being some sort of moral criminal. And looking at it like that tends to make it more difficult and even seem dumb.

Is it? Let's skip to the bottom line and look at results. If God really does know what is best for us and his laws are intended to guide us toward real happiness, then the results ought to show that, don't you think?

They do. Very few persons who have waited for sex until their "with you only . . . forever" person have later felt it was dumb, or felt they were cheated out of some excitement they should have captured while the chances were there.

But a lot of people who *haven't* waited later found that it was a mistake, that it was actually a waste, that it messed up their lives in some way. How many are in *that* position?

How large a calculator do you have?

Chastity — the Way of True Love

Waiting. It's called "chastity." The word has an old-fashioned ring to it for many people, but a lot of really great things have an old-fashioned ring to them — Christmas, for example. Such things are not great *because* they are old-fashioned. They have lasted for centuries simply because they're great. Being old or new has nothing to do with it.

Chastity may not be too popular with the media, but it is or will be with your "with you only . . . forever" person.

"Some people think it doesn't really matter to a girl any-more whether or not her guy has waited, whether or not she is the only one. Boy, are they wrong," a girl told me.

Chastity. Waiting. Is it a dumb thing to do? Is it a waste of opportunities that won't come again? Is it just a matter of obedience to an old rule, so that parents (and maybe God) won't get bent out of shape?

Not quite.

Preparing a gift, a magnificent gift — that's what it is. If you have ever really, *really* worked to prepare a special gift for someone — planned it and spent time on it and worked hard for it because you wanted it to be as special as possible, because you wanted to make someone as happy as you could — you have some idea of what you are really doing when you wait.

Is it easy? No way. Is it worth it? Ask someone who has been there . . . who has been given a "with you only . . . forever" gift.

"I love you — completely, unreservedly. From among all the people on earth, I choose you to give everything I have. . . ."

What a neat thing to be able to say.

5

The Pressure of Peer Pressure

There's a song by a rock group called "Lord, Is It Mine?" The final verse, done in the group's best driving, rhythmic sound, trails off unexpectedly with the line, "There must be a thousand voices trying to get through."

Do you feel sometimes there are "a thousand voices trying to get through" . . . to you? Maybe there aren't a thousand, but enough, at least, to make it confusing and sometimes a hassle: parents and grandparents; brothers and sisters and other relatives; teachers and counselors and coaches; religious authorities, civil authorities, doctors, and advice columnists.

All of these together, however, are often in the minority. At least they do not seem as strong as one other single group — your friends.

Sometimes they are not all friends in the strict sense of the word — you would not entrust them with your personal feelings nor choose to spend a two-week vacation with them. But they are a part of your life. They are your classmates, your teammates, the kids in your neighborhood, the group you go with. Unless you are practicing twenty-four hours a day to be a hermit or a lighthouse keeper, you have to deal with them and with the peer pressure they bring into your life.

That is not always easy to do. But sometimes people talk as though it were: "Well, just don't pay any attention to what everybody else thinks." This advice is usually well-meant, but it often sounds about as practical as, "Don't pay any attention to that tickling in your nose. Just decide you are not going to sneeze, and ignore it."

Peer Power

Peer pressure does not affect only young people, and it is not exactly new. Remember Nicodemus and Joseph of Arimathea from the gospels? Both were at least middle-aged and both were rather certain that Jesus had the handle on what life was about. But they kept their admiration and faith pretty much to themselves for quite awhile. Why? They were scared of what *their* peers would say or do. It's a familiar story. As far as we can tell, both of them eventually did bring their faith out of the closet and did not get sidetracked by peer pressure.

But it doesn't always work that way.

It didn't work for a kid I'll call Tony. Tony is nineteen, and he is in a place called a "correction facility." That is the *nice* name for it — you can get pretty sick to your stomach listening to stories of what really goes on in there. Unfortunately, it is quite possible that Tony will come out a lot more messed up than "corrected" or "rehabilitated" or any of those nice-sounding names.

Why is he there? You could answer that in several ways, but you would have to include the names of a half dozen other guys about Tony's age. They did not *force* him, at least not physically, to do what he finally got busted for. But at the time, Tony thought they were the coolest people on earth; so when they were into this or that, Tony was with them all the way. It wasn't that he didn't know better or that he was a born jerk. "He just got in with the wrong crowd," Tony's parents say today.

How many other parents, brothers, sisters, and friends are saying the exact same thing about other good kids — kids who got tragically sidetracked by peer pressure? I hate to think.

And here is the kicker: *Where are* all those guys Tony once thought were so important that he had to adopt their values, their life-style? One is also doing time. Four have moved away. One is dead. (He got drunk and totaled both his car and himself.) *The people over whom Tony messed up his life are no longer even in his life.* You can call it ironic or call it the pits or call it a waste. They all fit.

"But that's an extreme example. Peer pressure doesn't always put people behind bars."

True. Peer pressure does not automatically manufacture criminals. But being behind bars is not the only way of having your life messed up.

Following Blindly

Our country has over five million outright alcoholics, and about five million more people who are "heavy" or "problem" drinkers. That is ten million people plus — whose drinking causes serious personal problems. How many do you suppose got started or were encouraged by "friends" who thought it was cool to get a really good buzz on?

How many young people miss out on a great — maybe lifelong — relationship with someone they would like to go with, but don't because their "friends" do not think that person is enough of a "hunk" or a "fox"?

An estimated one million young people run away from home each year. Some run away because they honestly feel life at home is intolerable. But many others do so because "friends" advise: "Hey, if you don't like it, man, cut out. There are lots of places to live." (There aren't, by the way. And runaways have three things they can do to survive: steal, deal, or sell themselves. Not too great a future.)

How many dropouts do you suppose there are whose peers convinced them that school was a waste? How many kids flunk or do badly in a major course because their peers think the teacher is a jerk — or that getting good grades in that course is a very uncool thing to do?

How many people have cut off their relationship with God because they finally gave in to "friends" who say, "You mean you still go to church"? How many young people have wasted the gift of their sexuality because "friends" said, "Hey, if you haven't scored by this time, there's something wrong with you"?

When we are talking peer pressure, we are not talking nickel-and-dime stuff. It's big. It can bring about difficult-to-change or even permanent directions in a person's life.

Real-life Fears

Why do people give in to peer pressure, even though they know it is leading them in a wrong direction? You could probably write a 400-page psychological study on that, but I think the bottom line would be this: *"I'm afraid that if I don't go along with it, I'll be unhappy* (or unpopular or left out in the cold)."

It is similar to heavy drinkers who know or suspect that they are headed in a dangerous direction but are afraid that if they stop drinking they will fall apart; that is, their problems will seem too big, they will not feel confident or optimistic, they will not have a reward, or there simply will not be anything to make them feel good. The drinking soon causes more problems than the unhappiness they are afraid of, but they do not see that.

The conformist thinks in the same vein: "If I stop going with the crowd, I'll be unhappy — people will call me names; I won't have any friends; I'll be laughed at."

Here, too, going with the crowd often causes more unhappiness and downers than the rejection the person fears. Among other things, a young person who always gives in to unhealthy peer pressure is constantly caught in a bind. On one side there's "What will my friends think if I don't?" And on the other side there's "What will my parents do if they find out that I did?" That is a pretty miserable place to be, when you think about it.

Persons and Puppets

"I don't know how to fight peer pressure," a young person said to me once. I think "fight" is the wrong word. We can learn a lesson from Jesus here. When some people were thinking of throwing him off a cliff, he did not charge at them with fists flying. He "walked through their midst" and went on with what he wanted to do.

And the first step is contained in those last five words. I wish we could print the following sentence in three-dimensional letters surrounded by flashing neon lights. ASK YOURSELF WHAT YOU WANT IN YOUR LIFE! God made you a totally unique, independent person. Don't serve that up on a platter to the crowd — most of whom won't have anything to do with the "permanent" part of your life: your career and your future family.

Jesus said to *care* for your friends and be of service to them. He did *not* say to let them run your life. He washed the feet of his apostles, but he never gave in to their negative thinking or lack of faith. There is nothing selfish or unchristian about being in charge of your own life. That is why God gave you a brain and a free will.

And if you are not sure what you want or how right or wrong something is, then you had better make a decision about it sooner rather than later. Think, pray, and decide as best you can. Because if you don't, there will always be someone in the crowd who will enjoy deciding for you. If there is a particular area where you feel pressure from peers and it leaves you uncomfortable or uneasy, take some time for yourself; think about it, and then decide: "If it were *strictly* up to me and no one else knew or cared, what would I do?"

If you are not accustomed to doing this, you have a pleasant experience in store. It is a lot nicer to feel like a person than a puppet.

Do It Your Way

I am not going to try to snow you into thinking that there is a totally effortless, painless, almost magical way out of peer pressure. Confronting a group that wants to do something you don't is never a piece of cake. But there are ways to make it smoother.

You can disagree with someone or with a group without putting them down and without preaching a sermon like some "Holy Joe." Make it known that you are exercising your right to run your own life, nothing more, nothing less. If you get static, ask why that person doesn't want you free to make your own decisions. (Some adults may not agree with me here. They may think you *should* stand up and give a formal defense of principle and virtue. I believe your simple, calm refusal to conform is sermon enough and actually more effective.)

You can take a hint both from Jesus and from the masters of the Oriental self-defense arts: Do not resist an opponent's force with pure, contrary force of your own — turn his force around to your advantage. You will be doing it verbally instead of physically. Let's look at a couple of versions of the same situation.

Group: Tonight let's . . . (whatever — but you'd rather not).
You: I don't think so.

Group: Why not? Chicken?

You: No, I'm not chicken.

Group: Sure you are. If you weren't, you'd do it. Check it out, everybody — look who's so nice and good all of a sudden.

You: I'm not trying to be good. I'm just . . . .

Group: Just chicken. A good, square, little chicken. And a little strange.

You: No, I'm not. You're the ones who are strange. And stupid.

OK, I think you can see this is going nowhere. The reason it is going nowhere is because in the example you are trying to put force against force, and the conversation is getting off the real issue at hand — your independence, your freedom of choice. Let's do a replay of it.

Group: Tonight let's . . . .

You: I don't think so. See you tomorrow, OK?

Group: Chicken to come with us?

You: Do I *have* to do everything you do?

Group: Check it out, guys — look who's chicken!

You: You afraid of answering the question? Do I *have* to do everything you do?

Group: You're a little strange, man.

You: That's not the point. I'm not telling you what to do or not to do. I just like running my own life. What have you got against that?

Keep the conversation centered on *your* right to run your own life. That is the point at stake. And don't let yourself be convinced of something that is not true by emotional words like "chicken." Such words are pretty relative, to say the least. You are not gutless if you choose not to get into a cage with a hungry polar bear. That is simply called having your head on straight. It is the same with other things people might try to get you into.

Maybe it seems like I have painted peer groups solely as a semi-hidden enemy. I don't mean that. The good times we enjoy with our friends are some of the best things God designed in this life. We can honestly hope that among the people we go with there will be those who will help, not hinder, our growth as persons, as Christians.

But you have to remember that sometimes people change when they are in a group. Sometimes the group takes on a not-so-great personality that none of its members have individually. People do things as part of a group which they would never do on their own. That is when you have to *think enough of yourself* not to follow where you don't really want to go.

People in your peer group: like them and love them but, if you need to, leave them — at least for awhile.

Tony wishes he had.

6

How to Pray When It's the Last Thing You Feel Like Doing

Let's invent a little kid. But don't tune out because our character is a little kid. Maybe he won't turn out to be so little by the time this is over.

We'll call him Iggy — short for Ignatius. Iggy has a sore throat, a fever, and general achiness. He really hurts, but he is trying to cover it all up because he doesn't want to miss having fun. Obviously, Iggy is fairly normal.

Into this situation, let's insert some sore throat, general achiness medicine. It's quite good; it's even guaranteed. It doesn't taste bad, either. In fact, once a person gets beyond the first swallow, it's really good. And it is exactly what Iggy needs right at this moment. His sore throat and achiness are getting worse, and he is not going to be cured without it.

But Iggy is positive the medicine will taste awful. He rolls his eyes into his head and makes a face at the thought of it. He is positive he won't be able to swallow a drop of it. Besides, it probably won't do him any good anyway. It might work for some other people, but not for him.

What a dumb little kid, right? He is turning away from the one thing he needs most. Well, even I have been a dumb little kid on more than one occasion. You probably have, too. Maybe we can learn something from our imaginary dumb little kid.

Excuses, Excuses

We do that a lot, you know; we turn away from (or don't even consider) the very thing we need most.

Take, for example, someone in good physical shape. Chances are that person likes to exercise. Someone who is out of shape, however, hates the thought of it. He or she may need the exercise even more, but it is immensely difficult to start. And such a person can dream up any number of excuses to avoid making that start.

"I'm going to feel dumb huffing and puffing around laps when I haven't even walked around the block lately. I won't be any good at it. It'll look phony and ridiculous."

"It's going to take a lot of exercise to get results. I don't know if I'm ready for that. If I don't see results right away, I'll probably get discouraged and quit. If I quit, I'll feel stupid for having started."

And the final, blockbuster excuse: "I'm probably too far gone anyway. I could exercise like crazy and still not get back in shape. I may as well live with what I've got."

Now it is exactly like that with praying. Just when talking with God is what we need most, it seems to be the most difficult, far-out, even dumb thing to do. And we use different forms of the excuses above to postpone or avoid it. Let's look at some of the situations where this happens.

1. "I'M NOT SURE I BELIEVE." You may not doubt the existence of God, you may simply be having trouble believing something he said or was supposed to have said. From where you are, you just can't see it. And when you're having trouble believing something *God* is supposed to have said, it feels awkward, to say the least, talking to *Him* about it. You figure he is going to be really upset with you if you question something he said.

2. "I DID SOMETHING WRONG. I BROKE GOD'S RULES." OK, maybe you broke lots of rules. This is a particularly scary situation. You imagine God to be a revenge-minded person, whose rules you have broken, or someone you have hurt. You are naturally afraid that if you come close enough to talk, you will get a triple-barreled shot of "You worthless turkey — what's wrong with you? Get out of here! It makes me sick just to look at you!"

So you choose a "cooling off" period. You figure that maybe after a few days or weeks or months, God will have mellowed a bit or forgotten what you did. In the meantime, maybe you'll straighten up your act enough to face him.

3. "I HAVEN'T BEEN AROUND IN AWHILE." This is where you haven't robbed any banks, haven't thrown hatchets at anybody, nor committed any particularly horrible sin. You have simply been very distant from God. You have been paying attention to a lot of other things, maybe almost everything *but* God. You do not deny that God exists, but he has been close to zero in your life.

This is another uncomfortable situation. You feel as you would in regards to a friend who has been loyal but whom you have ignored and avoided for no good reason. You expect to hear, "You've got a lot of nerve coming back after all this time and expecting things to be the same!"

So again you put it off. You wait for a time when, for some reason or other, everything will be cool again. Maybe, then, praying will come as easily as turning on the stereo.

The problem is that you really need contact with God *now*. It is never too late from God's point of view, of course, but if you wait too long, you may decide it is a lost cause. (Like the person who figures he is so out of shape there's no sense even starting to exercise, remember?)

What do you do in situations like these? How do you pray when prayer seems . . . well, you know.

You Don't Have to Snow God

First, you scrap the cover-up. If you saw the movie, *Oh God!,* you probably remember the scene where John Denver is reluctant to step out of the shower because God (George Burns) is standing right there. God tells him, "Oh, come on, you think I don't know what you look like?"

It's sort of like that. God is the *one* person you don't have to play games with or pretend for. He already knows it all. Now that may be scary in one way, but it is actually comforting and relaxing in another. For example, if you are honestly confused about something in your faith, you do not have to snow God into believing that your problem is honest and real and that you are not just putting on a show or being stubborn about it.

When you have messed up and have to confront the person in charge, it is difficult to be straight. You feel you have to spin some whitewashing garbage like, "It wasn't really my fault, see. I couldn't help it. I didn't know what I was doing. Besides, it wasn't that bad." This can be anywhere from uncomfortable to nervewracking. You wonder if you sound convincing enough, and you worry about how the other person will react. With *God,* you can say, "I really messed up. And I'm confused about why. And I'm afraid it might happen again if I'm not strong enough." Unloading that kind of honesty is a positively refreshing change of pace.

With a friend whom you have neglected, you might not be sure what kind of reception you will get when you try to reestablish connections. With God . . . well, you know the Prodigal Son story.

God Won't Zap You

It is a wonderful feeling not to have to play a role or search for snowy words and phrases or cover anything up or worry if the other person understands your side of things. With God you can use gut-honest words, words that might stick in your throat otherwise. At first they may not be so easy with God either, because you are so used to covering up. But it becomes easier.

So if there is something that you are supposed to believe but you have a real, honest difficulty with it, you tell God that.

Tell *God* that? God? Right!

Do you know anybody better equipped to help? What is he going to do — zap you with lightning for being honest?

This is assuming, of course, that you are being straight. If you try to do a slick little number on God, to con him into something, it won't work. But if you are playing it straight with God, there is nothing he won't do to help you.

Try reading chapter nine in Mark's Gospel, starting with verse fourteen. You will find a man who wasn't sure whether Jesus could help or not. I don't know whether the man doubted Jesus or his own worthiness to be helped. Maybe it was both. In any case, Jesus did not exactly have your classic, A-1, solid gold, super-faithful believer standing in front of him. But the guy had the guts to talk to Jesus anyway.

Did Jesus give up on him? No. He threw the man a challenge, not a rejection. And then, in verse twenty-four, the man blurts out a gut-honest prayer. It is translated in various ways. A traditional version reads, "I do believe. Help my unbelief." Today he might say something like, "I do believe . . . kind of. But not like I guess I'm supposed to. Help me sort it all out."

Precisely when praying may be the last thing you feel like doing, when praying may seem like a loser, you have everything to win by trying it.

7
A Candid Look at Pornography

This chapter is for anyone who finds "dirty pictures" at least a little bit . . . interesting. That is an honest, up front opening. I am not just trying for a cheap but surefire attention getter.

We could pretend that every single one of us finds every single one of "those" pictures absolutely hideous and disgusting. We could pretend that if the following page featured a spread of nude bodies, all of us would instantly snap our eyelids shut, rip the page out of the book, burn it, and find the whole experience revolting.

While we're at it, we could also pretend that we have eliminated prejudice, wiped out poverty, established worldwide peace and justice, and overcome all the effects of original sin. So let's not pretend, OK?

True, terribly extreme or abnormal pornography is disgusting to everyone except the genuinely sick and perverted. But not everybody would rip a centerfold out of a magazine and burn it in horror. Some would have a difficult time closing the magazine or turning the page — not just "dirty old men" or perverted demons or "kids with sex on their minds all the time" either. Some good, Christian people who basically try to be straight with God would be tempted.

Nothing Evil about Beauty

What about this "I know it's a dirty picture but I still want to look" situation? If you find yourself in it, what does it say about you?

Perhaps surprisingly, several good things are *trying* to work in this situation. Yes, I said *good* things. Notice I also said trying, not succeeding. (It is something like the case of a superbly designed sports car roaring the wrong way down a busy one-way street. The car is beautiful. What might happen is not.) These are the good things:

1. THE HUMAN BODY REALLY IS BEAUTIFUL. That's it: pure, plain, and simple. Painters and sculptors have celebrated this fact since the days of the caveman. People who find the human body repugnant or embarrassing have something wrong with them. There is nothing evil about being able to appreciate human beauty. But if we have our heads on even a little bit straight, we will also realize that this beauty carries an element of possible danger with it. Beautiful things often do.

2. ATTRACTION is a different matter and beyond simple appreciation of beauty. Finding the body of the opposite sex attractive is also a very good thing. That ought to be so obvious that it should not have to be noted; but, unfortunately, our sexuality acquires a lot of "guilt by association." The massive misuse of sex begins to make otherwise level-headed people feel there is something embarrassing or not too nice about the whole male/female setup. (These people sometimes try to impose a silence about the subject, often disguising their embarrassment by saying, "Something as holy as sex shouldn't be talked about.") But the actual attraction someone feels, even in a so-called dirty picture, is not dirty in itself — at all.

3. HUMAN BEINGS ARE NATURALLY DRAWN TOWARD CLOSENESS, toward intimacy with others. This is again a good thing. We instinctively want to discover others' secrets and to share our own. It doesn't take much imagination to see how this revealing and discovering, this sharing of closeness,

can be attempted simply by revealing and looking at the body itself.

God's Impossible Rules

So if you find it difficult to turn past the centerfold in a "skin mag," those three good things, three God-designed human qualities, are *trying* to happen as they were planned. They are not succeeding, but trying. That is important to understand. If you don't, you may get a couple of conflicting and confusing opinions bouncing around in your head. One will say, "You're just normal, that's all." The other will say, "You've got a warped, perverted, dirty mind."

That is a dangerous situation, too. If you feel "dirty" and "bad" from something that at the same time also seems to be a normal instinct, you might just plain give up on being good. This is one of the devil's favorite situations. It is a perfect spot for him to plant this idea: "See? God's rules are impossible! If you are normal, you are going to break them. It's automatic. So why fight it? You might as well go ahead and enjoy yourself."

OK. So finding "those" pictures tempting, then, doesn't mean you are rotten. So maybe the whole bit with pornography is pretty normal and human, and really not so bad? That is about as close to the truth as *Star Wars* is close to *Romeo and Juliet.*

"Lilies That Fester . . . "

Like many evils, pornography is a case of something beautiful gone terribly wrong — and that makes it all the more horrible. If you don't mind a little Shakespeare tossed among the centerfolds, he had a line that really says it: "Lilies that fester smell far worse than weeds." In other words, the more beautiful something is when it goes right, the more awful it becomes when it is perverted and misused.

What is really wrong with pornography? For starters, let's take the words of Jesus: "Anyone who looks lustfully at a woman has already committed adultery with her in his thoughts."

Now that is rather blunt. But Jesus had a positive habit of calling it like it is. And he was making a point that is extremely easy to overlook: If something is wrong, it is wrong whether or not you get burnt officially and publicly for doing it. There is a law against rape, for example, but you will never get busted for looking at pornographic pictures. However, Jesus seems to link the two (the action and the thought) rather closely together.

A Matter of Theft

Pornography is a sharing of something nobody has a right to share. Lingering over a pornographic picture is, literally, taking something we have no right to take.

"But I didn't force anyone to pose for the picture, and I didn't snap the shutter or print the magazine. And if I don't buy the magazine or look at the pictures, it won't make any difference — it will still be there."

That is true as far as those facts go. But let's say you are passing a store that someone has broken into. Yes, somebody *else* originally broke in. Other people have already come by and taken what did not belong to them. Still others will probably come along after you and do the same. Whether or not *you* walk in and take something won't change any of that. Is it OK?

You know the answer to that one.

It isn't *what* you might take that is bad. It might be, in itself, wonderful and beautiful. But it is wrong to take it when you have no right to it.

Pornography and Sexual Crime

Besides being wrong in itself, pornography leads to more wrong. Some people might say, "I look at those pictures, sure, but they don't, you know, have that much effect on me." Jesus would tell them to knock off the nonsense and start being honest. It is difficult, if not impossible, to look at pornography without soon wanting to do considerably more than look.

Few, if any, people in the country know this better than Simon Leis, Jr., the chief prosecutor of Hamilton County, Ohio. Mr. Leis is nationally known for his successful prosecution of *Hustler* magazine and for ridding Hamilton County of several chains of pornographic bookstores. Does he see a direct connection between pornography and sexual crime?

"Definitely, positively, beyond question," Mr. Leis asserts. "There are many cases where the fact of pornography is literally part of the crime." He cites one gruesome case after another wherein, by the defendant's own confession, the urge to commit a crime came directly from viewing pornographic material. In many cases, the actual idea (often for violent or unnatural sex) came from the pornographic material itself.

"The effects of pornography are not restricted to criminal court," Mr. Leis adds. "Sit in on any domestic relations court, talk to any marriage counselor," he suggests. Many marital problems, he claims, are created or aggravated by one or both partners indulging in pornography.

The Destruction of Society

What is the biggest single negative effect of pornography? Mr. Leis does not hesitate for a second in answering that.

"Nothing less than the destruction of society. It's a rather simple case of cause and effect," he says. "Pornography attacks the family. When the family is destroyed, society is in chaos."

OK, somebody might still say, "So porn isn't the nicest thing around, but it's still hard to see how it's really *that* bad. Because, after all, an awful lot of people. . . ."

There it is: "If a lot of people do it, want it, accept it, it just can't be too wrong."

Really?

A lot of ancient Romans thought it was OK for men to kill and torture each other, for wild animals to devour screaming human beings, for women to be mass raped . . . all for their public amusement in the Colosseum.

A lot of people in ancient Greece thought homosexual relations, particularly between men and young boys, were OK.

In our own century, a lot of people saw little wrong with the methodic murder of over six million Jews.

In some places until recently, a lot of people thought human sacrifices and cannibalism were just part of life.

"Lots of people do it" shows only one thing: It is possible for lots of people to be terribly, drastically wrong.

. . . like when they say pornography really isn't all that bad.

8

"Be Yourself" vs. "The Church Says"

A wonderfully honest young person recently mentioned a problem she had with religion class and the Church.

In religion class, she kept hearing the advice, "Be yourself." On the other hand, she pointed out that the Church keeps telling us what we are supposed to believe and how we are supposed to act. Isn't there a huge conflict between being ourselves and being Catholic?

If you have similar feelings now and then, keep a couple of thoughts in mind: You are not the first to have them, and you are not a rotten, religiously uncool being in the sight of God, either. (God is far more understanding of us than we are of each other.)

Quite a few people experience a "Be yourself vs. the Church says" hassle from time to time. Let's see if we can sort it out a bit.

No Answer Sheet

First, this whole religion thing — God, Church, Good, Evil, Sin, and Salvation — is B-I-G. It is quite a few steps up the ladder from, let's say, the multiplication tables where things have been rather settled for centuries and are unlikely to change. Whereas we — the Church — will *always* be challenged to deepen our knowledge of God and sort out what he has revealed to us. Jesus did not pass out mimeographed sheets to the apostles right before the Ascension and say, "OK, guys, this is it. Every answer you will ever need is right here."

Secondly, religion touches us very personally and deeply. Whatever bottom line we arrive at in religion, if we take it seriously, is going to affect drastically the way we live. It is quite a few steps up the ladder from, let's say, choosing a brand of peanut butter.

So it should not be at all astounding if the pieces of the "religion, Church, and my life" puzzle do not always fall neatly into place.

And when they do not, you have to avoid three very tempting but wrong conclusions: (1) You can't ever make sense out of religion anyway, so why try? (2) The Church is dumb. (3) Maybe I'm not a very good person. If I were good, I would not be having problems and doubts.

We Christians, and maybe we Catholics in particular, have somehow been saddled with an unrealistic view of ourselves. Deep down, we feel we should never have disagreements, doubts, or differences as far as our Church is concerned, at least not major ones. This just isn't so. Life is not like that. Read the Acts of the Apostles in the Bible and you will find it was not like that in the early days of the Church either.

Unfortunately, if you think that way, then when disagreements or doubts do come up, it always seems like somebody has to be wrong — otherwise the hassle wouldn't take place. On the other hand, if you can get rid of that "some turkey has to be at fault" outlook, your problems as a Christian will be a lot more manageable.

Unlimited Freedom?

It is always enjoyable to hear advice like "be yourself" and similar versions like "dare to be different." Such advice seems to be saying, "Step out into unlimited freedom . . . anything you think, say, or do is just fine."

That sounds really attractive — like an exciting free fall through space without ever having to worry about hitting the ground or getting airsick.

Unfortunately . . . you guessed it! It just isn't that simple. There is no such thing as an unrestricted, unending free fall through space. It might be a great trip if it could be arranged, but it can't — and you would probably start wishing for stable, familiar scenery sooner than you think.

Anyone who advises you to be yourself — a religion teacher, a counselor, whoever — should also explain that being yourself does not mean you can forget or ignore anything anybody else ever tells you. It *can't* mean that. And it's not because some group (the Church, the city, the school) gets a power trip of their own out of taking away your freedom and telling you what to do, but because with no limits or guidelines for being yourself, life is not livable.

If I decide that being myself includes playing my stereo — whether Beethoven or the top twenty rock hits — at top volume early in the morning, I am going to make life unlivable for my family and/or my neighbors.

If I enjoy golf but spend nearly every single spare dollar and minute on it and become a stranger to my wife and kids, that is not right. And it cannot be defended on the grounds that "I'm just being myself. I'm a golf freak. That's just the way I am."

Shouldn't I come to realize for myself, on my own, that my family is being hurt? That would be ideal. But what if I *don't* see it that way on my own? What if I think all this golf is perfectly normal and OK — what happens then?

My wife and kids keep getting hurt. That's what happens. I need somebody to help me see things the way they really are.

In fact, it would have been a good thing if somebody had pointed this out to me *before* I created the situation.

God's Design for You

It may help you to consider some of the Church's rules in this way. The Church isn't really a dictator shouting, "This is how you are going to act . . . Why? Because I said so, that's why!" If you have met some individual who does come on that way, just remember he or she does not represent the way Jesus wanted his Church to act.

It is more like someone (and someone who cares) saying, "Hey, you're going to get yourself messed up, or you'll hurt other people if you act this way or that."

The Church tries to pass along God's design for you. And God's design is not just a set of dumb rules he made up to see if you can take it. God is not, for example, a really tough soccer coach who says you have to run twenty extra laps just to see how obedient you are. God's rules are there because he knows what is good and what will actually make you happy when it comes to the bottom line. (Have you ever noticed how many people who have so much money and power that they can do anything they want — or almost anything — end up miserable?)

A Need for Rules

So what does it mean to be yourself? Is it nothing more significant or exciting than choosing a brand of peanut butter? Do teachings and rules get in the way of being yourself? Some examples may help.

In soccer you are not allowed to use your hands to pass the ball or score a goal. Does that keep you from being an exciting soccer player and developing a style of your own? Of course not. In spite of dozens of rules in any sport, coaches and players are constantly developing new patterns and strategies. In fact, that is exactly what makes it exciting. If every player were free to decide for himself or herself how to play the game, all sports would be: (a) not much of a challenge; (b) not much fun; and (c) pretty dangerous.

There are literally thousands of rules for writing, for example, covering everything from spelling to grammar and punctuation to the elements of a good novel. In spite of them — or rather, actually by *using* them — people continue to create new stories, articles, poems, plays, and books every year — each one different from any other that has ever been written.

Being yourself is something like that.

Three Steps in Sorting It Out

What happens if all this sounds fairly OK, but you still have a problem with this or that particular teaching of the Church?

1. Try as well as you can to figure out *why* you have a problem with it. This is called keeping yourself honest, and it is something everybody has to do. Do you experience a genuinely upsetting wrestling with the problem or would you just prefer it weren't there because your life would be easier that way? You need to make sure you are not acting like someone who argues that it is stupid to have first base so far away from home plate because it would be easier to get on base if it were closer.

2. If your problem is real and genuine and honest, you need to realize that the people with whom you disagree are not the enemy. And they, of course, should realize that you are not the enemy either.

3. You pray about it. A lot. Not "Lord, please give me victory over those stupid turkeys who can't see how dumb they are," but "Lord, I'm having trouble with something that I know is fairly important. I need your help to sort it out. And, Lord, please help me 'day by day, to see thee more clearly' and still be myself."

9
The Great Turn-on Chase

If you have read the novel *Tuned Out* by Maia Wojcie-chowska (I can't pronounce her name either, but she's a good writer), you may remember the scene where Kevin, just back from his first year of college, is trying to persuade his younger brother Jim to join him in getting stoned.

"A pot smoker is a pleasure-seeker," Kevin tells him.

Jim isn't into pot, and he challenges his brother on the pleasure angle: "But you're not happy."

At this point, Kevin makes a really profound statement: "I didn't say you get happiness from pot. I said pleasure."

Pleasure vs. Happiness

As strung out and burned out as Kevin is, he still sees the difference between pleasure and happiness.

Sometimes the words are used as synonyms, but they're not. People might argue over the precise distinction between the two ideas, but the following descriptions fit the point Kevin was making in *Tuned Out.*

Let's use "pleasure" to mean a good feeling that is often heavily physical or a combination of physical and emotional. Some pleasures are almost strictly physical, like good things to eat and drink. Some are more mental and emotional, like watching a good movie. Maybe the simple all-purpose word "fun" comes close to what we mean here.

Happiness is more difficult to capture in words. We might do better to list some results or signs of happiness. Among other things, you are happy when:

— you wake up and really want to get started on the day, even if it is a workday or school day;

— you think life in general is good rather than a real drag with a few high-spots;

— you feel deep down that you are an OK, worthwhile person;

— you do not spend a lot of time wishing things were different.

Pleasure and happiness are not opposites or in conflict with each other — they are simply not the same thing.

What Price Happiness?

But doesn't pleasure bring happiness? If you stuff your life full of enough pleasures, won't you be happy? It is easy to think that way. You are bombarded with messages telling you that if you wear designer jeans, ride in a great set of wheels, go to enough parties, drink a certain brand of beer, eat deluxe pan pizza, see all the latest movies, and shove quarters into the video game machine, you will be happy. True?

No. Take Kevin in *Tuned Out.* He is turning on all the time — and he is positively miserable. Kevin is fictional, of course, but it is not unusual to read about people in real life who are rich and powerful enough to buy any imaginable pleasure — and are miserable. They can get an unlimited amount of anything from gourmet food to expensive booze to luxurious surroundings to sex. And at the end of it all, they put a gun to their heads or tell a reporter how lousy their life has been.

Does pleasure always bring happiness? The record shows otherwise.

The Anti-fun Image

If you sense a "Stop Having Fun So You Can Be Holy" message coming, forget it. I am not on that bandwagon.

In fact, it is unfortunate that religion often gets saddled with an anti-fun image. A few people in the history of Christianity have done a lot to promote this image, even though they were probably sincere at the time. Way back in the third century, a fellow called Manes started a thing, later called Manichaeism, which considered the human body bad news. In the seventeenth and eighteenth centuries, a thing called Jansenism taught that people were all slaves of desire for sinful pleasure — and nearly every pleasure, of course, was sinful.

Closer to our own times, the Puritans picked up on this idea. Now I really admire those strong-willed old Puritans for a lot of things. But their "Practically Anything Enjoyable Is Bad" notion was off track.

And finally, every now and then we come across a picture of a saint with a facial expression that seems to reflect a severe case of acid indigestion.

For some people, all this adds up to one conclusion: "Holiness may be a good thing to have in the next life, but in this one it's a real drag."

That is simply not true!

For one thing, it does not square with what God tells us in Scripture. Let's look at the Garden of Eden story in Genesis, the first book of the Bible. We know that this Genesis account is not so much intended to relate what happened on a certain date in super-ancient history; rather, it is intended to be a picture of *how people are* — how *we* are, how we handle the situation we are in.

The situation: God places human beings in a pretty wonderful world. There are lots of good things around, if they look for them. God draws some limits, but as the Genesis story indicates, there are more fun things than there are no-no's.

What do the human beings do? Right away they want to cross the foul line. They are so interested in what is off limits that they ignore what isn't. The banishment from Eden tells them that if they are so terribly interested in what is on the other side of the foul line, life is going to be a hassle.

Balancing It All Out

God's original idea, though, is still true. Insofar as we can live with it and keep our heads on straight, life is supposed to be generally enjoyable and enjoyed. (Caution: This is not the same thing as a lifelong, carefree, responsibility-free, non-stop party.)

There is more evidence in the Bible for the same idea. Among other things, Jesus put together his first miracle at Cana simply to keep a wedding reception from breaking up too soon to the disappointment of all and the embarrassment of the bride and groom. He also said, "If a man wishes to come after me, he must deny his very self, take up his cross . . . ." (Are you picking up a pattern here? Life is meant to be neither nonstop party nor nonstop pits. It is a mixture, or perhaps better, a rhythm.)

Pleasure and fun certainly do not deserve the "Evil, Wicked Stuff" label that many people have tried to pin on them. But they are not exactly harmless, either. They can and do get us into trouble.

A few so-called pleasures are just plain wrong by themselves — always. For example, some people get a sick trip out of being cruel to others. Nothing will ever make that OK.

Sometimes a pleasure is wrong because of the situation or the circumstances. Casual, for-kicks-only sex is an obvious example. But sometimes it is not so obvious. Example: What about spending the afternoon at the pool — an OK thing? Of course. But supposing company is coming for dinner. Mom is already tired from doing the laundry. She could really use some help to straighten the house and put the whole occasion together. Taking off for the pool in this situation suddenly becomes pretty selfish.

Pleasure becomes a monster when our pleasure-seeking is nonstop. We lose the idea of life as a rhythm — periods of genuine (and hopefully meaningful) work alternating with periods of letting loose and having fun. We start wanting life to be a full-time turn-on, a never-ending party. This is called going back to our childhood. A three-year-old wants only to eat, drink, play, and feel good all day long, every day. This is normal — if we are three years old. When a teenager or an adult wants only to eat, drink, and play all day and every day, it is pretty sad.

Too Much of a Good Thing

Nonstop pleasure-seeking also invites dependency and addiction. Those words usually make people think of alcohol and other drugs. And for a good reason: Chemical highs really grab hold of human bodies and leave an "I want more!" message when they drain away. But almost any pleasure can turn into a monster. It takes over one's life and throws it off balance. People can become addicted to television, the stereo, poker, video games, or growing African violets. The solution is not to put a ban on fun. The solution is to have one's head on straight going in and keeping it that way.

Finally, there is TGIF in hyper-drive. This is where you realize that life cannot be a nonstop party — but still, partying is the *only* thing that means anything to you. It is the *only* thing you enjoy. You drag through the week for one reason only: to get to the weekend. And when you get there, you knock yourself out trying to soak up enough pleasure to make up for the nowhere week you just had.

What is sad about this is that you see little or no value in three-fourths of your life, maybe more. And if you see no value in it, you are not likely to give it your best shot. Therefore, you don't accomplish much. You feel bored or hassled or both, and you really go nuts waiting for another weekend or the next party. The cycle keeps repeating itself.

And the worse you feel about your regular life, the more you try to spice it up when fun-time does come. At this point you are a good candidate for messing yourself up by *over-doing* your letting loose.

A Little Like Fertilizer

What is the bottom line on pleasure? I am not sure how to give a nice, neat bottom line. Pleasure is not the enemy; it is not thoroughly evil, wicked, and rotten. But it is not the solution, either; it won't make you happy all by itself. You have to check to make sure your desire for pleasure isn't messing up other parts of your life.

Maybe pleasure is a little like fertilizer. I know that's a pretty far-out comparison, but in a way it really fits.

If you have a plant that is already healthy, some fertilizer here and there will make it better. But too much fertilizer will burn the plant out — just plain kill it. If the plant is really sick or dead, no amount of Super-Hi-Turn-On-Wonder-Gro is going to bring it to life or make it healthy.

In the same way, if your life is already basically happy, some doses of fun will make it even more enjoyable.

Nonstop partying will burn it out.

And if your regular, ordinary life is not generally worthwhile and rewarding, no periodic, temporary turning-on will ever bring you happiness.

10

The Put-down/Put-away Challenge

Imagine it is your first day at a new school. You arrive late and hurry to your first class. Everybody else is already there.

You open the door of the classroom and gasp for breath. What you see inside is like a scene from a far-out movie. It is almost too weird — no, too sick — to watch; but you do so anyway with a sort of morbid fascination.

The people in the room are methodically slapping, punching, sometimes even kicking each other. It isn't that an all-out fight is going on. In fact, the atmosphere is relatively calm for the most part; people are going about their regular business. But every now and then somebody goes over to somebody else and delivers a slap in the face. The slap is not forceful enough to knock the person down or rearrange the cheekbones, but more than enough to hurt. Some people hear the sound of the slap and look up, some do not. Those who do notice smile or laugh at the incident. At times the person who was slapped hits back, but not always. Sometimes, instead, he or she goes over to an entirely different person and delivers a punch or a kick.

Everybody is hurting. But no one says, "Let's stop." No one even questions why they are involved in this insanity. That is the mind-blowing part: They seem to accept this as *normal, routine* behavior! It is as though all this deliberate hurting and being hurt is actually expected.

Weird, weird, weird, right? In fact, this is "El Sicko" in hyperdrive. Call the wagon and the guys in the white suits; carry these people off and get them some help, right?

It Happens in Other Ways

Have you ever witnessed a scene like that in real life? Believe it or not, you probably have. It happens quite a bit. It isn't done physically with slaps and punches and kicks, although sometimes that can happen as a result. Rather, it is done like this:

"You're stupid." "What a wimp!" "How'd you get to be so ugly?" "Use your brain for a change." "What do you know about anything?" "You always screw everything up." "You're fat." "You're scrawny." "You fag." "Shut up." "Get lost." "Jerk!" "Creep!" "Ass!"

Why? WHY?

There are lots of reasons, and they are all like spokes coming out from one central, underlying biggie. Before we talk about that biggie, let's eliminate something we are *not* concerned with.

We are not talking about friendly kidding, the affectionate "insults" that happen between people who like each other. (Most of my friends like to needle me about the "glare" from the spreading bald spot on the front of my head. I explain that the heat from the intense brain-wave activity directly underneath is responsible.)

It is difficult to put into words a precise description of the difference between friendly kidding and deliberate or thoughtless put-downs. Frequently, almost the very same words could be used for both. Rather, it is the occasion or the tone of voice that makes the difference. But I don't think we really need to define the difference precisely. We *know* the difference. We can tell friendly kidding from unfriendly put-downs. Here we are talking strictly about the latter.

The Put-down People

There are those who might say, "Put-downs don't bother *me.* I don't care what people say or think" — but I will never buy that. It might be true coming from a robot made of steel and wires and plastic, but not from a person. We can get used to hearing put-downs, but that is not the same thing as being unaffected by them.

We usually assume that people who put others down a lot are really stuck on themselves. They apparently think they are so big and bad, so much better than everybody else. They must have egos like King Kong has a body.

Wrong. Absolutely . . . dead . . . wrong!

If I am tempted to take something away from you, it is probably because I do not think I have enough of whatever it is. If, for example, you drop a five dollar bill without noticing it, I may be tempted to pick it up and keep it — if I don't have as much money as I think I need. That, in itself, will not force me to take the money, but I may be tempted.

But let's say I have a few hundred thousand stashed in the bank, plus some stock, some real estate, and all the ready cash I need. Again, you come along and drop your five dollar bill. Am I tempted? No way! I don't *need* the five bucks. Your Aunt Gertrude can send you a couple thousand or so for your birthday, and that won't bother me either. I have as much as I need. *I am satisfied with me.*

This is true of more than money. It also works in regards to the way we feel about ourselves. The only reason we would want to make another person look or feel small is because we do not feel tall enough ourselves.

The bottom line is this: The real reason for a put-down is a not-too-super image of oneself.

Portrait of a Loser

Put-downs are a losing venture all around, because they do not really make the person who dishes them out feel better. If I score a real zinger on you, I may feel the thrill of a cheap victory for a few minutes, but it doesn't last. It doesn't last because it is not real. Instinctively, my gut tells me that I am not actually any taller or better just because I put you down.

A put-down is only a quick fix for the bad feeling I have about myself — quick and very short-lived. Soon I need another one. I need to put somebody else down. It is like trying to fill up on iced tea when I am starved for a full meal. That "full meal" will come only if I do something that makes me feel OK about *me* . . . all by myself, and not in comparison to anyone else. If that never happens, I will probably keep trying to feed the empty spot inside me with more and more not-very-satisfying put-downs. What does a diet like that produce?

Losers! And that's a shame. Because God made us to be winners — all of us.

In the Winner's Circle

If I feel OK about myself and my own life, I will want the other person to feel the same way. Someone who is healthy does not need a quick, sick fix that comes from making another individual feel rotten. Take a good look at some of the winners who are in the national limelight. Look at the people who win Super Bowls and Oscars, Pulitzer and Nobel awards, or even Miss America contests. I am not saying that these awards are the most important things that happen on this planet, but someone has to be a winner to get there. What do these same people say about others — even about their own competition?

They say good things. They give compliments — that's what. And they are not phony compliments, either. They are real ones, born of genuine respect. These people do not feel uncomfortable or uneasy in saying that somebody else is good . . . or even better. For years sportswriters argued over whether Bradshaw or Staubach was the best of the active professional football quarterbacks. Whom did these two themselves choose? They chose each other. The other guy was the best. And they did so out of genuine and mutual respect, not phony humility.

Winners feel so good about themselves that they like to spread that feeling around. They know it will not be lost by being shared.

There are many different kinds of winners. Some of them wear Super Bowl rings, while others cannot afford half the price of a Super Bowl ticket. But one thing is true of them all: You will not hear them putting other people down. Losers do that. Only losers need the quick, sick fix of making somebody else look or feel bad.

The Jesus Way

This does not mean you have to be all hearts and flowers, nonstop sugar and sweetness. It does not mean you never call it like it is, never raise your voice in anger, never blow the whistle on something wrong or set somebody straight in very direct, blunt terms. There are times when you *have* to do that, when you actually have an obligation to say some harsh words, make waves, and rock the boat.

But none of those things is the same as put-downs. They are not even in the same ball park.

Was Jesus all hearts and flowers? Hardly. Check out Matthew 11:20-24 and 12:34-37 or Mark 7:1-13. There are similar passages throughout the Gospels if you look for them.

And don't forget that whole "cleansing of the Temple" scene in Matthew 21 and Mark 11 — not exactly the gentle approach. When Jesus saw an evil situation, he said what he had to say, and his words were not always dripping with syrup. But he never put people down just for the sake of putting them down — his whole purpose was to raise them up, to help them become the best they could be, to help them to become winners.

You can join the winner's circle, too. Accept the challenge to put away put-downs by taking the following pledge now:

I am accepting the challenge to feel good about myself — by making others feel good about themselves.

I will say good things about other people, unless there is an obligation to point out something that's wrong. I will be a winner by making others feel like winners. Only losers want others to feel like losers.

I will not try to build my self-image by putting others down. Only losers do this. I will not fake strength by calling others weak. I will not fake intelligence by calling others dumb. I will not fake ability by pointing out others' mistakes. Only losers do this.

I am fine all by myself. I do not need to tear down somebody else's life in order to build mine. I do not need to make others look little in order to make myself feel tall. I do not need to make someone else feel worthless in order to make myself feel worthwhile.

I am a winner!

Other helpful publications from Liguori

Getting in Touch with Jesus
by Brother Joseph Moore, C.S.C.
The goal of many young people today is to get to know Jesus. This book offers solid guidance for today's teens and twenties. Each chapter is followed by a "spiritual exercise" designed to help young people become involved in Christian witness, social awareness, and deeper spirituality in personal relationships. *$2.50.*

How to Develop a Better Self-image
by Russell M. Abata, C.SS.R., S.T.D.
A beautiful "self-help" book that should lead to self-discovery, self-control, and a greater acceptance of self, others, and God. Blends practical psychology with a Christian view of life. Written by a priest-counselor. *$2.50.*

The Sacraments Today: Their Meaning and Celebration
by Christopher Farrell, C.SS.R., and Thomas Artz, C.SS.R.
This book takes a fresh look at the sacraments, explaining each one and pointing out that they are *true signs of love* between God and man. Once understood, the sacraments come alive as truly *personal meetings* with Christ. *$2.95.*

Sexual Morality
Guidelines for Today's Catholic
by Russell M. Abata, C.SS.R., S.T.D.
A straightforward discussion of sex, giving rights and wrongs and reasons why. Covers such subjects as the desire for sex, the relationship between sex and love, and the need for moral guidelines. The last chapter is a beautiful essay on sex and God. *$1.50.*

Should You Become a Priest?
by Reverend Terence E. Tierney

Should You Become a Sister?
by Sister Marcella Holloway, C.S.J.

Should You Become a Brother?
by Leo Kirby, F.S.C.
These thoughtful, compelling booklets offer information and insight into religious life today. Each booklet centers on a particular calling and seeks to answer the question: "Should you become a priest?" ". . . a Sister?" ". . . a Brother?" *Each — $1.50.*

You and the Ten Commandments
by Russell M. Abata, C.SS.R., S.T.D.
A set of nine booklets that explain the place the Ten Commandments have in everyday living, emphasizing the positive. These booklets show how the commandments fit into your hectic pace and the changing style of modern living. *Complete set — $7.95.*

Your Faith
A Redemptorist Pastoral Publication
A comprehensive study of Catholicism, from Jesus' Jewish background to a study of each sacrament. Includes illustrations and pictures interspersed with the fast-moving, readable text. Ideal for all high-school grades and young adult programs. *$2.95.*
Leader's Guide available — *$2.95.*

Order from your local bookstore or write to:
Liguori Publications, Box 060, Liguori, Missouri 63057
(Please add 50¢ for postage and handling.)